PROPERTY OF
ST. CLEMENT'S
LIBRARY
ROSEDALE, MD.

WWII

PEARL HARBOR

WORLD

TURNING
POINTS OF

PEARL
HARBOR

WILLIAM E. SHAPIRO

A GROLIER COMPANY

FRANKLIN WATTS ■ 1984
NEW YORK ■ LONDON ■ TORONTO ■ SYDNEY

Picture research by Roberta Guerette, Omni Photo Communication
Photographs courtesy of:
Culver Pictures: pp. 6, 18, 48, 65;
UPI: pp. 8, 27, 30 (top and bottom),
42, 45, 58, 61, 62, 76, 78.

Maps courtesy of Vantage Art.

Library of Congress Cataloging in Publication Data

Shapiro, William E.
Pearl Harbor.

(Turning points of World War II)
Includes index.
Summary: Traces events leading up to and resulting
from the December 7, 1941, Japanese attack on
American battleships at Pearl Harbor, which brought
the United States into World War II.
1. Pearl Harbor, Attack on, 1941—Juvenile literature.
[1. Pearl Harbor, Attack on, 1941. 2. World War, 1939-
1945—Causes. 3. Japan—Foreign relations—United States.
4. United States—Foreign relations—Japan]
I. Title. II. Series.
DS767.92.S43 1984   940.54′26   84-7324
ISBN 0-531-04865-9

CONTENTS

WWII

PEARL HARBOR

CHAPTER

PEARL HARBOR: THE PLACE, THE EVENT

Far out in the Pacific Ocean, some 2,500 miles (4,000 km) from California, lies the United States' youngest state—Hawaii. The United States annexed Hawaii in 1898, made it a territory in 1900, and brought it into the Union as the fiftieth state in 1959.

Hawaii consists of eight main islands and 124 smaller ones that stretch across 1,500 (2400 km) miles of the central Pacific. If you were to approach the islands from the east, where all eight main islands are located, the sixth island you would see is Oahu, the third largest in the chain. Oahu is called the Gathering Place, and it is indeed the center of Hawaiian life. Eight out of every ten Hawaiians live here, and the state's capital, Honolulu, is on the southern coast.

Oahu is dominated by two mountain ranges that run from the southeast to the northwest. Between them is a beautiful and fertile valley that is planted with pineapples for as far as the eye can see. The small streams in the south, such as the Pearl Stream, flow down from the mountains, cross the lush valley floor, and empty into Pearl Harbor. With ten square miles of navigable water, Pearl is one of the largest and best-sheltered natural harbors in the entire Pacific. It has been the home of the United States Pacific Fleet since the spring of 1940.

Around the perimeter of Pearl Harbor there are dry

PEARL HARBOR

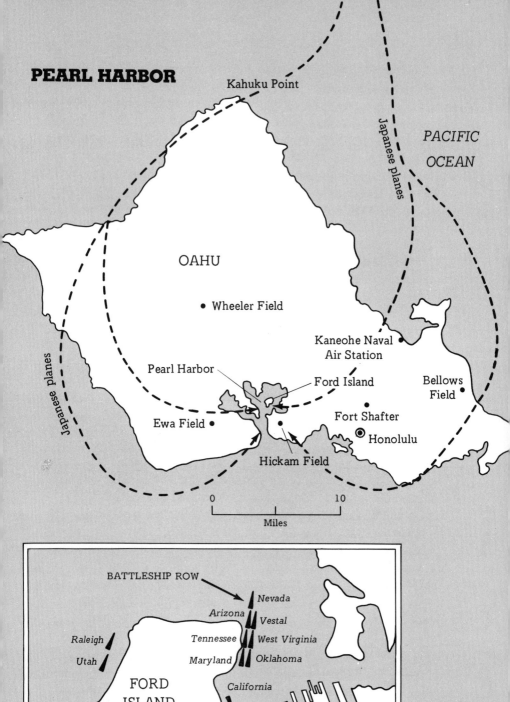

Kahuku Point

PACIFIC OCEAN

Japanese planes

OAHU

● Wheeler Field

Kaneohe Naval
Air Station ●

Pearl Harbor

Ford Island

Bellows
Field ●

Japanese planes

Ewa Field ●

Fort Shafter ●

◎ Honolulu

Hickam Field

0   10
Miles

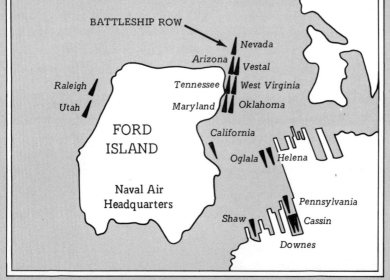

BATTLESHIP ROW

Nevada

Arizona   Vestal

Raleigh

Tennessee   West Virginia

Utah

Maryland   Oklahoma

FORD
ISLAND

California

Oglala   Helena

Naval Air
Headquarters

Pennsylvania

Shaw   Cassin

Downes

docks and naval yards, oil storage tanks and depots. A submarine base is in the northeast corner, as is Pacific Fleet headquarters. In the center of the harbor sits Ford Island. The waters around Ford Island are the deepest in the harbor, and the largest ships of the United States Fleet—the battleships and carriers—have long anchored here. Today, side by side with these big ships, a special memorial floats above the broken hull of a battleship that died there in 1941. The *Arizona* was one of six American battleships lined up like sitting ducks in Battleship Row when the Japanese attacked Pearl Harbor in the early morning hours of December 7, 1941. Twelve hundred American sailors were killed when the *Arizona* went down.

The Japanese attack was carried out by hundreds of carrier-based planes that bombed, torpedoed, and strafed the Pearl Harbor Naval Base as well as other American military installations on the island of Oahu. In just two hours, more than 2,400 Americans were killed and 18 ships and 188 airplanes were destroyed. The loss might have been greater. Fortunately, the three aircraft carriers attached to the Pacific Fleet were not at Pearl Harbor on that fateful morning.

The defense of Pearl Harbor was at times gallant. But the attack was totally unexpected. As a result, American sailors and soldiers were able to shoot down only twenty-nine of the attacking planes and destroy one submarine and five midget submarines. Fewer than one hundred Japanese were killed.

When the attack started at 7:55 A.M. in Hawaii, it was nearly 2:30 in the afternoon on the east coast of the United States. At that time, on that Sunday afternoon, countless Americans were listening to the radio broadcast of the Giant–Dodger football game. The broadcast was interrupted, and the announcer informed the American people of the stunning news. The nation looked to Washington for its response. It came on the following day, when President Franklin D. Roosevelt addressed a joint session of the United States Congress:

*The Japanese view of Pearl Harbor on the
morning of December 7, 1941.*

Yesterday, December 7, 1941—a date which will live in infamy—the United States was suddenly and deliberately attacked by the naval and air forces of the Empire of Japan. . . . The attack yesterday on the Hawaiian Islands has caused severe damage to American naval and military forces. Very many American lives have been lost. . . . I ask that Congress declare that since the unprovoked attack by Japan on Sunday, December 7, a state of war has existed between the United States and the Japanese Empire.

Thus, the United States went to war with Japan, and three days later Germany and Italy, Japan's Axis allies in Europe, declared war on the United States.

When the United States went to war, war had already been raging in other parts of the world. The Japanese had invaded China in 1937 and were still trying to subdue that nation. In Europe, World War II had started on September 1, 1939, when Nazi dictator Adolf Hilter unleashed the German armed forces on Poland. Now, in December 1941, Hitler and his European ally, Italian dictator Benito Mussolini, controlled most of Europe. In western Europe, Great Britain, a close American ally, stood alone; in eastern Europe, the Soviet Union was fighting for its life.

The United States had been giving increasing military aid to Great Britain, but many Americans were against this. They felt that by helping Great Britain, the United States would be drawn into the war. In December of 1941, a great debate raged between those who wanted to aid the British and those opposed—the isolationists.

On December 7, 1941, the debate ended. There were no isolationists who wanted the United States to stay out of the war at all costs. There was only a united nation of 130 million people dedicated to the defeat of the Axis Powers—Japan, Germany, and Italy. Their rallying cry was "Remember Pearl Harbor!"

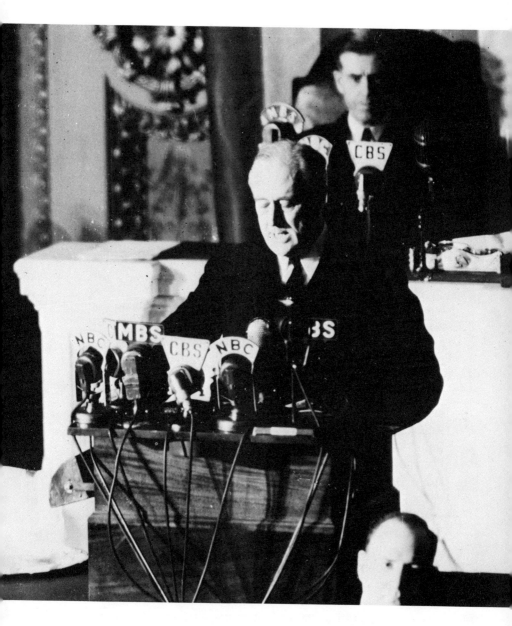

President Franklin D. Roosevelt, asking
Congress for a declaration of war against Japan.

Why did Japan attack Pearl Harbor? Whey did it risk war with the United States? For many years the Japanese had been intent on building an empire that stretched from Japan in the north to the East Indies in the south and from China in the west to Micronesia and Melanesia in the east. There was but one obstacle to Japan's ambitious plans—the powerful United States Pacific Fleet. The Japanese hoped to destroy this fleet.

The Japanese were successful at this. From a tactical point of view, their attack on Pearl Harbor was one of the most brilliant operations in military history. Their fleet had sailed, undetected, for thousands of miles through the waters of the North Pacific. They had caught the United States unprepared and destroyed a major portion of its fleet. They had, at the same time, mounted military campaigns to seize British and Dutch possessions in Southeast Asia, as well as the Philippines and Thailand.

But from a strategic and political point of view, the Japanese had committed a major blunder. By attacking the United States, they ensured, in the long run, their own defeat.

There were many Japanese leaders who had opposed war with the United States. Even Admiral Isoroku Yamamoto, the architect of the surprise attack on Pearl Harbor, had warned that Japan would never be able to defeat this industrial giant. And now the United States turned its industrial might toward preparations for war. Never before had any nation produced the machines of war in such staggering quantities. In four years of war, American industry would produce nearly 300,000 war planes, 71,000 naval and merchant ships, 86,000 tanks, and 315,000 field-artillery guns.

And the American people would unite as never before. Some sixteen million men and women would serve in the armed forces. Millions more would go to work in the defense industries.

For Japan, then, Pearl Harbor meant initial victory but ultimate defeat. For the United States, it meant that a united people would harness the nation's awesome industrial might and, for the second time in a quarter of a century, fight in a world war. And from this war the United States would emerge as the most powerful country the world had ever seen.

But now, on December 7, 1941, the American people were not thinking about the end of the war. Their thoughts were on Pearl Harbor. How, everyone wondered, could the United States have been caught napping? Didn't the nation's military and political leaders know that a Japanese attack was imminent? And if they didn't, why not? How could a Japanese fleet of more than thirty ships have sailed for thousands of miles, from Japan to Hawaii, without being seen? Who was responsible for this day of infamy?

There were not—and are not—easy answers to these questions. Many accused, and still accuse, President Roosevelt of keeping news of the imminent attack a secret, so that the United States would be drawn into the war alongside Great Britain. Others laid all the blame at the feet of the two highest ranking military men in Hawaii: Admiral Husband E. Kimmel, commander in chief of the U.S. Navy's Pacific Fleet; and Lieutenant General Walter C. Short, commander of the U.S. Army units in Hawaii. But no two individuals alone could have been responsible for a disaster of the magnitude of Pearl Harbor.

There were, indeed, many reasons why the Japanese were able to mount a surprise attack on Pearl Harbor. Among them was poor judgment on the part of American military and political leaders. For example, military cryptologists had broken the Japanese diplomatic code, yet the information obtained from intercepted messages was never analyzed correctly. Nor was it passed on to Kimmel or Short.

False assumptions on the part of military and political leaders were also responsible for the Japanese success at Pearl Harbor. Japan would not attack the United States, they said, because its goal was to take over British and Dutch possessions in Southeast Asia. This was indeed the Japanese goal. But so far as Japan was concerned, the United States would try to prevent this from happening, and thus the United States Fleet would have to be destroyed.

In 1941 the United States and Japan were on a collision course, a course that the United States had helped determine less than one hundred years earlier, when it had forced Japan to open its ports to trade with the United States.

EARLY
JAPANESE-
AMERICAN
RELATIONS

When Marco Polo returned to Venice from China in 1295, he brought with him great treasures and wondrous tales of Kublai Khan's Mongol Empire in eastern Asia. He also brought news of a land no European had ever heard of before. Marco Polo called it Cipango—"the land where the sun rises"—but not until the great Age of Discovery would Europeans make their way there.

In 1543, while the French and Spanish were exploring the wilderness that would one day become the United States of America, a Portuguese ship reached one of Cipango's (Japan's) southernmost islands. The men aboard were the first Europeans ever seen by the Japanese. Soon Portuguese and Spanish trading vessels were frequenting Japanese ports, and Jesuit missionaries were busy converting the Japanese to Christianity.

For nearly one hundred years, the Japanese shoguns (military rulers) tolerated the foreigners, who now included the Dutch and English. The very substantial trade that had developed with Europe was to their benefit. And they learned a great deal about firearms and fortifications from the Europeans. But the Japanese rulers soon began to fear the power of the Europeans. European ships, they saw, were far superior to those of Japan. They could sail faster, and their cannons could easily destroy Japanese cities and coastal fortifications. What would prevent the Spanish or Portuguese from bringing an army from Europe and making Japan a colony? What would prevent the Spanish or Portuguese from promoting a rebellion against the rule of the shogun? Perhaps the Christian converts would rise up against the shogun.

Because of these fears, the Japanese decided to expel all foreigners from their country. This was accomplished by 1638. No foreigners were to be allowed back in, and no Japanese would be allowed to leave. (Only the Dutch, who had never attempted to convert the Japanese to Christianity, were permitted to maintain a trading post on a small island in Nagasaki harbor.) Japan, in effect, went into a self-imposed state of isolation from the rest of the world. This isolation would last for more than two hundred years.

The first American contacts with the Japanese took place around the turn of the nineteenth century, just a quarter of a century after the founding of the United States. At first these contacts involved only the supplying of the Dutch trading post by American ships. But as the nineteenth century progressed, more and more American sea captains sailed their merchant ships into the waters of the western Pacific Ocean. Their clipper ships called at ports of trade in China, and their whalers pursued the 50-foot-long gray whales of the North Pacific.

Many American sailors became shipwrecked in the stormy seas of the North Pacific, and some of them ended up on Japanese soil. The Japanese would not allow these sailors to return to the United States. Many of them were mistreated and some were killed. When word of this reached the United States, the government became determined to contact the Japanese to discuss the fate of the sailors. Spurred on by commercial interests, the government also wanted to discuss the use of Japanese ports for the refitting of American ships. Japan's location, near the Asian mainland as well as the whaling ground, made it ideal for this. But during the 1830s and 1840s, several American attempts to discuss these matters with the Japanese were rebuffed.

In 1851, however, an increasingly more powerful and confident United States decided to become insistent. The government made plans to send a naval squadron to Japan to force the issue. Now, in addition to discussing the fate of American sailors and the use of Japanese ports by American ships, the United States government also planned to force the Japanese to open their ports to trade with the United States.

Soon after sunrise on July 8, 1853, four American naval vessels sailed into Tokyo Bay. All four of them were painted black, and two of them, outfitted with steam engines, belched black smoke from their stacks. These "black ships," as the Japanese called them, were commanded by Commodore Matthew C. Perry, an aristocratic, no-nonsense Navy officer. His mission was to deliver a letter from President Millard Fillmore to the Japanese demanding that Japan open its ports to trade with the United States. Perry delivered the letter and told the Japanese that he would return for their answer in the following year.

Perry returned in February 1854—this time with a larger fleet. There were eight warships, three of them steam-driven, and two supply ships. On board the ships were two thousand marines and sailors. Dozens of guns and cannons were visible to the Japanese who watched this impressive fleet sail into Tokyo Bay.

The American display of force was not lost on the Japanese, whose naval forces, after two hundred years of isolation from the now-industrializing nations of the Western world, seemed woefully antiquated. The Japanese agreed to sign a treaty with the United States. The Treaty of Kanagawa, signed on March 31, 1854, opened two ports to trade with the United States. It also assured that American sailors shipwrecked near Japan would receive humane treatment and that American ships could call on certain Japanese ports for supplies and to be refitted. Japan's two hundred years of isolation had come to an end.

The Japanese soon signed similar treaties with a number of European nations. But within Japan, many people resisted

*Commodore Matthew C. Perry lands at
Gorahama in Tokyo Bay in 1853.*

these renewed contacts with foreigners. In a number of violent incidents, Americans as well as other nationals were killed. American ships were fired on, and the American and British legations were burned down.

Many of these acts were committed by the subjects of a group of daimyos (feudal lords) who opposed the Tokugawa government and who wanted to rid Japan of all foreigners. Tokugawa shoguns had ruled Japan in the name of the emperor since 1603—the emperor had little or no real power. The daimyos forced the shogun to resign, and the emperor again became the ruler of Japan. This event, in 1867, ushered in a new era in Japanese history.

The years from 1867 to 1912 were known as the Meiji era, or Enlightened Rule. The emperor, whose name was Matsuhito, was also known as Emperor Meiji. Instead of getting rid of all foreigners, he called on the Japanese to learn as much as they could from the nations of the West. The ensuing years were marked by a headlong rush by the Japanese to assimilate as much Western knowledge and technology as they could. They embarked on crash programs to make their military forces as modern as those of the West. They poured huge sums of money into building an industrial base. They streamlined their government and their banking system. Their educational system was revamped, using the American system as a model. Students by the thousands were sent to schools in other countries, primarily in the United States. In less than fifty years the Japanese would transform their country—a feudal state would become the leading power in all of Asia. One historian called this "the most remarkable achievement in the history of the modern world."

During the Meiji era, Japan was helped most in its modernization programs by the United States; it sought to emulate the United States more than any other country. Ironically, its rise as the foremost political and military power in Asia would coincide with the United States' rise as a great Pacific power.

In 1848, following the American victory in the Mexican War, California became part of the United States. Two decades later, in 1867, the United States purchased Alaska from Russia. To many, this acquisition was "Seward's Folly," but to Secretary of State William H. Seward, it was a giant step forward in his goal of extending American influence into the Pacific and Asia. Even as it acquired Alaska, the United States annexed the Midway Islands in the central Pacific. Seward urged that it should annex the Hawaiian Islands as well.

The United States did not annex Hawaii in that year, but it did sign a commercial treaty with its rulers. This brought Hawaii into the American sphere of influence. Three years later the United States signed a similar treaty with Samoa and obtained the right to build a naval base at Pago Pago. The United States was rapidly becoming a nation with vital interests in the Pacific. But while the government was certain that this was a desirable step, the people were not. They had fought a terribly destructive civil war just a decade earlier, and they now feared that expansion into the Pacific could lead to armed conflict with other nations.

This attitude on the part of the American people would soon change. In the 1890s, as the nation rapidly industrialized, the people came to realize that foreign markets were needed for American goods. They also came to believe that trade with other nations, especially those of Asia and the Pacific, would necessitate the establishment of military and naval bases in these areas. At this time, there was great interest in Charles Darwin's theories of evolution and the survival of the fittest. Many people suggested that Darwin's ideas applied not only to animals and human beings but to nations as well. The American nation, these people believed, was racially superior to other nations (especially non-white nations) and was destined to rule the weaker peoples of the world. James G. Blaine, who served as secretary of state from 1889 to 1892, under President Benjamin Harrison, did not support this theory. But he did believe in the need to strengthen the United States' position in world affairs. He and President Harrison continually sought to build naval bases in the Caribbean and the Pacific. Like Seward two decades earlier, Blaine also favored annexation of Hawaii.

American influence in Hawaii had begun in the early 1800s, and by mid-century Americans dominated the economic and political life of the islands. The United States and Hawaii signed a trade agreement in 1875. Twelve years later King Kalakaua—the Merry Monarch—gave the United States permission to build a naval base at Pearl Harbor on the island of Oahu. Kalakaua died in 1891 and his sister, Liliuokalani, became queen. But she believed in "Hawaii for the Hawaiians." In 1893, in a revolution led by Americans and supported by Blaine, Liliuokalani was forced from the throne. A short-lived republic was established. Then, in 1898, the United States annexed Hawaii; in 1900 it became a United States territory.

The end of the nineteenth century was a major turning point in American history. The nation became a colonial power. Not only did it annex Hawaii, it acquired—by one means or another—Samoa, Guam, Wake Island, and the Philippines. The increasingly more powerful United States Navy roamed the waters of the Pacific to protect the nation's newly acquired empire.

Japan, too, was building an empire, or at least beginning to. In 1894-95 it defeated the Chinese and took control of Formosa (today's Taiwan) and the nearby Pescadores, a group of sixty islands in Formosa Strait. Japan also ousted China from Korea and became the protector of that nation. In 1905 Japan defeated Russia in the Russo-Japanese War and took control of the Liaotung Peninsula in southern Manchuria, which Russia had controlled, and the southern half of Sakhalin Island.

Up to this point in time, Japanese-American relations were relatively good. But after the Russo-Japanese War, relations began to deteriorate. Many Japanese believed that the Treaty of Portsmouth, which ended the war and which had been engineered by President Theodore Roosevelt, had deprived them of a complete victory over the Russians. The two nations also clashed over China. The United States championed the Open Door Policy, which gave all nations equal trading rights in China. Japan opposed this. Discrimination against Japanese living in the United States, especially those on the west coast, also increased anti-American feelings among the Japanese.

Japan, which had learned the benefits of empire building from the United States and the nations of Europe, continued its expansionist policies. In 1910, it annexed Korea. And in 1914, after the outbreak of World War I, it seized a number of Pacific island groups that had been part of Germany's colonial empire. These included the Marshalls, Marianas, and Carolines. At the end of the war, Japan kept these islands as League of Nations mandates.

By the early 1920s, Japan had the most powerful navy and strongest army in Asia. In the view of the American government, it was also the only nation that was trying to upset the status quo in that part of the world. As a result, the United States government felt threatened; it felt that the Japanese were trying to undermine its position in the Philippines.

The American people, however, had no intention of going to war to protect United States interests in this area. They had enthusiastically supported war efforts during World War I because they had felt that they were engaged in "a crusade to make the world safe for democracy." But this was the roaring twenties, the golden twenties, and the energies of the American people were directed inward. They wanted, above all, to avoid all foreign entanglements and to concentrate instead on reaping the benefits of the booming American economy.

CHAPTER III

FROM
ISOLATION
TO STEPS
SHORT
OF WAR

Despite the isolationist sentiments of the American people at the start of the 1920s, the United States government was growing increasingly concerned about events in the Far East. It was especially concerned about Japan's growing strength. As a result, it invited Great Britain, Japan, France, and other nations to a conference in Washington, D.C. The conference began in November 1921 and ended in February 1922. The attending nations agreed to respect each other's rights with regard to their possessions in the Pacific Ocean. They also agreed to guarantee China's independence and territorial integrity.

There were also military agreements, which included a limit on the size of each nation's navy. According to a formula worked out, the Japanese could have three major naval ships for every five major American ships and five major British ships. This seemed to indicate that the Japanese would have a smaller navy than either the United States or Great Britain. But the numbers were misleading. Both the United States and Great Britain operated fleets in two oceans. The United States also kept a sizeable segment of its fleet in the Caribbean. The Japanese fleet, in contrast, was centered only in the Pacific and, as a result, the Japanese maintained naval supremacy in that area.

But despite this outcome, the Japanese were unhappy.

They felt slighted because their fleet would be smaller than either the American or British fleet. Japan placed most of the blame for this situation on the United States. Adding fuel to the fire, in 1924 the United States passed a law formally excluding Japanese immigrants from the United States. The Japanese took this as a national insult. Anti-Americanism was rampant in Japan, and Japanese-American relations sank to a new low.

Events in China worsened the situation. The Chinese had overthrown their emperor in 1911 and established a republic, but the real rulers of the country were military men called warlords. Each warlord ruled over his own area of China, and the central government had no real power. Sun Yat-sen, who had been the first president of the republic and who was now leader of the Kuomintang, or Nationalist Party, tried to unite the country, but he died in 1925 before succeeding. One of Sun's followers, Chiang Kai-shek, became the Nationalist leader. Chiang, a military man, was able to defeat most of the warlords, and in 1928 he united China under one government. Japan viewed a united China as a threat to its dominant position in the Far East. It also viewed the United States as China's major benefactor. The Japanese leaders faced this threatening situation by turning to war.

In 1931, while Chiang was fighting the Communists for control of China, Japan invaded Manchuria, China's northernmost province, and turned it into a Japanese-controlled state called Manchukuo. A year later, the Japanese attacked the Chinese city of Shanghai and in 1933 took control of the province of Jehol, making it part of Manchukuo. The United States government gave Japan a verbal lashing for these actions and refused to recognize Japanese control of Manchuria. But the American threats had no force behind them. The American people would not sanction any military efforts to free Manchuria from Japanese control. Nonintervention in the affairs of other nations was still an overriding principle of the American people.

Japanese forces fighting in Manchuria undergo uniform inspection before moving to the front lines.

The Stock Market crash of 1929 and the Great Depression that followed had reinforced the isolationist views that had developed after World War I. With economic hard times upon them, the American people felt an overwhelming need to concentrate on solving their own problems. In addition, Japan's invasion of Manchuria, Mussolini's nationalistic ravings in Italy, and Hitler's rise to power in Germany in 1933 convinced them that the world order was collapsing. They wanted no part of such a world. Here was a world, they felt, in which businessmen and bankers, munitions makers and politicians were responsible for wars. To support this belief, they pointed to the 1934 Nye Committee report which showed that many American businessmen had made fortunes during World War I.

Franklin D. Roosevelt took office as the 32nd president of the United States in 1933 at the height of the Great Depression. At this time Roosevelt shared some of the isolationists' views. In 1920 he had espoused American membership in the League of Nations, but now he opposed American membership in the world organization. The League, he felt, had not lived up to its potential for keeping the peace. As if to underscore Roosevelt's feelings, Japan withdrew from the League after it had condemned Japan's invasion of Manchuria. The condemnation was the extent of the League's actions; it was powerless to take any further action.

A year later, in 1934, Japan announced that beginning in 1936 it would no longer abide by the naval agreements of 1922. Japan, it was obvious, was accelerating its drive to control eastern Asia. The United States ambassador to Japan, Joseph Grew, warned Washington that Japan's plans included the domination of China, the Philippines, and British and Dutch possessions in Southeast Asia. Its plans, he said, would include military force as well as diplomacy.

In 1935, Hitler began to rearm Germany in violation of the Versailles Treaty that ended World War I. Mussolini's Italy invaded Ethiopia, a poor and backward country in eastern Africa, in that same year. In 1936 Hitler reoccupied the Rhineland, civil war broke out in Spain, and Hitler and Mussolini announced the formation of the Rome-Berlin Axis. A year later Japan invaded China. Ambassador Grew's assessment had proved correct. Japan was now intensifying its effort to become the dominant nation in eastern Asia. This mineral-poor nation was striving to obtain raw materials by force. And it was striving to dominate the political, economic, and cultural life of eastern Asia by force. To many in Tokyo, there was only one country that could thwart Japan's plans—the United States.

During Japan's invasion of China, many Americans were killed. This, and reports of Japanese atrocities against the Chinese people, resulted in a rise of anti-Japanese sentiment in the United States. But when an American gunboat, the *Panay*, was sunk by Japanese planes in December 1937, the United States government did little more than protest. The Japanese wisely apologized for the incident and compensated the United States for the loss of lives and the ship. They were unprepared at this time for a military confrontation with the United States. A confrontation, however, would have been unlikely. The American people, a poll showed, wanted American ships out of China so that there would be no chance of war. The 1930s was the decade of the dictators, and the American people feared that once again their country would be drawn into a conflict.

The Congress, alert to the mood of the nation, enacted several pieces of legislation that were designed to forestall such a likelihood. The Neutrality Act of 1935 forbade the export of war equipment to either Italy or Ethiopia, and a year later loans or credits to Italy were prohibited. In January 1937, Congress banned the export of munitions to both the Nationalists and Loyalists who were fighting in Spain. In May 1937, yet another act required that nations at war pay on delivery for raw materials bought in the United States.

The government, however, did not invoke the Neutrality Act in the case of Japan and China. Its intention was to leave the door open for China to purchase oil and raw materials.

But China lacked the money to do this, so Japan was helped much more than China. It continued to purchase in the United States much-needed raw materials and industrial goods, which fueled that nation's war machine. In the year following its invasion of China, Japan bought from the United States more than ninety percent of its scrap iron, steel, and copper. It also obtained two-thirds of its oil and nearly half of its lead from the United States.

At this juncture the United States, while still intent on keeping out of foreign conflicts, recognized the need to strengthen its military forces. "World lawlessness is spreading," President Roosevelt warned the American people in October 1937. And in January 1938, in his annual message to Congress, he called for the expenditure of many billions of dollars for defense. For this request, Roosevelt was dubbed a "warmonger" by the isolationists, but many other people supported his stand. In May, two months after Germany invaded Austria and made it part of the Third Reich, the Naval Expansion Act authorized the building of a strong two-ocean navy at a cost of more than $1 billion. In January 1939, four months after Nazi Germany took over Czechoslovakia's Sudetenland and four months before it conquered all of that nation, Roosevelt asked Congress for an additional $2 billion for the military.

On September 1, 1939, German armies overran Poland. Two days later, Great Britain and France declared war on Germany. World War II had begun. In the United States a great and frequently bitter debate arose between the isola-

The American gunboat Panay *(above) at its standardization trial in 1928 and (below) sinking in the Yangtze River after an attack by Japanese planes in 1927.*

tionists and those who wanted the United States to aid the European nations that were attempting to resist the onslaught of Nazi Germany. The supporters of the Allies believed that if Hitler went on to conquer all of Europe, the United States would be next to fall. President Roosevelt, too, was firmly convinced that the proper course for the United States was to help the British and French and, at the same time, continue building up the American armed forces. Isolationists continued to argue that the United States should remain aloof from the wars of other nations. They wanted the United States to build its defenses but feared that giving aid to the Allies would lead the nation into war.

Who were the isolationists? They were a diverse group, and most of them were patriotic Americans. They included many businessmen from the Midwest who disliked Roosevelt and his New Deal. They included Italian-Americans whose sympathies were with Italy even though they did not support the fascist policies of Mussolini. Irish-Americans were also prominent among the isolationists, primarily because of their dislike of Great Britain for its policy toward Ireland. Pacifists were among their ranks, as were conservatives whose fear of the Soviet Union and Communism was greater than their fear of Germany and Nazism. There were also pro-Nazis like Gerald L.K. Smith and Father Coughlin, as well as members of the German-American Bund. American Socialists, led by Norman Thomas, opposed American intervention in any form. And the Communists were isolationists until Germany invaded the Soviet Union in June 1941. Then they became strong advocates of American aid and intervention.

In September 1940, many of the isolationist groups merged into the America First Committee. It had 800,000 members, and it had two goals: to persuade the American people that isolationism was the best course for the nation; and to try to influence Congress and the government so that no laws were enacted or steps taken that would jeopardize the peace of the United States. Charles Lindbergh was the Committee's most important spokesman. With the few exceptions noted above, America Firsters were not pro-Nazi or pro-Hitler. But to many Americans they often appeared to be defending German interests and German actions. The fact that they tended to ignore the German invasion of Denmark, Norway, Belgium, Holland, and France in the spring of 1940 alienated many Americans. The fall of France, especially, was a horrific event to most Americans. And it certainly ended the popular American misconception that Britain and France could defeat the Germans.

The most important group to oppose the America First Committee was the Committee to Defend America by Aiding the Allies. This group, like the America First Committee, wanted the United States to increase its military strength and to stay out of the war. But it campaigned for aid to Great Britain in the belief that if Germany were victorious, the United States would have to fight. The Committee to Defend America by Aiding the Allies had vigorously applauded President Roosevelt in June 1940 when he had stated that the United States would "extend to the opponents of force the material resources of this nation. . . ."

Meanwhile, President Roosevelt continued to request sizable sums for the United States military. In January and May of 1940 he asked for more than $4 billion for defense spending, including the production of more than 50,000 airplanes a year. Congress responded by approving a record increase in military spending, and in the summer of 1940, as the Battle of Britain raged, it approved the first peacetime program of compulsory military training in American history. The goal was to train two million soldiers, sailors, airmen, and reservists in one year. The Selective Training and Service Act, which was enacted on September 16, resulted in a first draft registration of 16,400,000 American men. But Congressional isolationists were successful in adding an amendment that barred the use of draftees outside the United States and its possessions.

As the United States armed itself, it also supplied huge quanitites of arms to Great Britain. In September the first of fifty destroyers was turned over to that beleaguered nation. The destroyers were followed by other types of naval ships as well as bombers. Once again, Roosevelt incurred the wrath of the America Firsters even though, in exchange for the destroyers, the United States was given leases on British naval bases in Newfoundland, Bermuda, the British West Indies, and British Guiana.

As 1940 ended and the Germans and Italians consolidated their successes in Western Europe, President Roosevelt set up the Office of Production Management. Roosevelt gave this agency a dual mandate—to supervise American defense production and to aid Britain and other anti-Axis countries in every possible way "short of war." The United States, Roosevelt told the American people on the eve of the new year, would become "the great arsenal of democracy." Now a steady supply of war matériel flowed to Great Britain. And when the British were unable to pay, Roosevelt proposed and Congress approved the Lend-Lease Act. The act enabled the United States simply to transfer military matériel to Britain and other Allies. American industrial might as well as moral right was now firmly pitted against the Germans, Italians, and Japanese. Eventually, Lend-Lease aid would amount to more than $50 billion and would be given to more than forty countries, including Great Britain, the Soviet Union, and China.

Roosevelt's "short of war" policy was of course designed to aid Great Britain. But it had another purpose as well. Roosevelt knew that by aiding the Allies he was gaining time for the United States to build up its military forces. He hoped, too, that these American actions would help restrain the Japanese. To further restrain the Japanese, Roosevelt now had a strong American fleet stationed at Pearl Harbor.

In the months following the approval of Lend-Lease in March 1941, the distinction between all aid to the Allies "short of war" and all aid to the Allies "including war" began to fade. In April, with the agreement of the Danish government-in-exile, the United States started to build military bases in the Danish colony of Greenland. The German and

Italian consulates in the United States were closed on July 7, 1941. And less than a month after the German invasion of the Soviet Union, on June 22, 1941, the United States sent military forces to Iceland to prevent that nation's occupation by German forces.

But it was the use of American merchant ships to deliver war goods to Great Britain that resulted in the first loss of American lives. An American ship carrying supplies to the British Isles had been sunk in May, and a destroyer had been attacked in the North Atlantic. Now, in September and October, the pace of attacks against American merchant ships and naval vessels quickened. A German submarine sank the U.S.S. *Reuben James* on October 30, killing one hundred American servicemen. This led Congress to authorize the arming of American merchant ships, a step severely criticized by many isolationists. The United States was one step closer to war in Europe. Six thousand miles away, in the Pacific, the signs were just as ominous.

Within two years of its invasion of China, Japan had conquered most of northeastern China. It also controlled all of China's important seaports. It now turned its attention to Southeast Asia, as Ambassador Grew had predicted years earlier. Japan, an island nation of some seventy million people, was woefully lacking in natural resources—especially resources such as nickel, iron, tin, oil, and rubber that are necessary for waging war. The United States was a major supplier of many of these raw materials. But for obvious reasons the Japanese were determined not to be dependent on the United States or on any other country. The answer, for the Japanese, was to seize areas of Southeast Asia where these resources were abundant. To Japan's leaders, Southeast Asia was the "Southern Resources Area." But this area was dominated by Great Britain, France, and the Netherlands. In June of 1940, however, France and the Netherlands were under the control of Germany. And Great Britain was preparing to fight for its life. Only the might of the United States stood between Japan and Southeast Asia.

In September 1940, Japanese troops moved into the northern part of French Indochina (what is now Vietnam). In that same month, Japan signed a military pact with Germany and Italy. This Tripartite Pact stated that if any one of these countries were attacked, the others would come to its aid. The United States viewed this pact as being directed against it. Indeed, at the end of 1940, the idea of war with the United States was no longer unthinkable to Japan's leaders. And Admiral Isoroku Yamamoto, commander in chief of the Japanese Fleet, had already conceived of a plan to attack and destroy the American fleet stationed at Pearl Harbor in the Hawaiian Islands.

CHAPTER IV

1941: THE BUILDUP TO PEARL HARBOR

Our Empire's plan to build a New Order in East Asia—the central problem of which is the settlement of the China Incident—is a firm policy. . . . The policy of the United States towards Japan is based on the idea of the status quo. . . . it aims to prevent our Empire from rising and developing in East Asia. . . . The policies of Japan and the United States are mutually incompatible. . . . The conflict will ultimately lead to war."

This Japanese policy statement was issued secretly for the guidance of government and military leaders. It was an accurate assessment of the conflicting aims of the two nations in 1941. Negotiations would be carried on throughout the year. But the United States and Japan would prepare for the war that to many seemed inevitable.

At the very start of 1941, the United States made it clear to the Japanese that if they wanted to establish friendlier relations, they, the Japanese, would have to remove their troops from China. There were at this time many powerful individuals within the Japanese government and military, especially the Navy, who did not want a war with the United States. But even they would never accede to the American demand that the Japanese give up China.

The inability of the two nations to resolve the China issue

strengthened the position of those who favored war. Yamamoto's plan to attack Pearl Harbor was now being discussed by a number of high-ranking military officers. Word of this reached Ambassador Grew on January 27 and he immediately notified Washington:

My Peruvian colleague told a member of my staff that he had heard from many sources, including a Japanese source, that the Japanese military forces planned, in the event of trouble with the United States, to attempt a surprise mass attack on Pearl Harbor using all their military facilities. He added that although the project seemed fantastic, the fact that he had heard it from many sources prompted him to pass on the information.

At about the same time, United States Secretary of the Navy Frank Knox wrote to Secretary of War Henry L. Stimson, expressing the view that "If war eventuates with Japan, it is believed easily possible that hostilities would be initiated by a surprise attack upon the Fleet or the Naval Base at Pearl Harbor."

Still, when Grew's message was read by Naval Intelligence, its assessment was that "no move against Pearl Harbor appears imminent or planned for the foreseeable future." Most Americans at that time would have agreed with this assessment. The Japanese, it was widely believed, were funny little people who were good at copying American goods, but they would never be able to stand up to the United States in a war. As one United States Congressman put it, "The Japanese are not going to risk a fight with a first-class nation. . . . They will not dare to . . . face the American Navy in open battle."

Indeed, in early 1941, the Japanese military was not prepared to take on the United States in the Pacific. Its fleet was more powerful and more modern than the United States fleet, but Japanese leaders feared that the minute their armed forces headed south and east, the Soviet Union would attack Japan from the north.

With this in mind, Japanese Foreign Minister Yosuke Matsuoka made plans to eliminate the Soviet threat. In late March and early April, he met in Berlin with Hitler and Joachim von Ribbentrop, the German foreign minister. The two did not share Matsuoka's fears about the Soviet Union. They strongly implied that in the near future, despite the Russo-German nonaggression pact, Germany would attack the Soviet Union. Attack Singapore immediately, von Ribbentrop urged. Matsuoka was promised German aid if the Soviet Union attacked Japan after Japan was at war with Great Britain and the United States.

These assurances from Germany were not enough for Matsuoka. He next traveled to Moscow, where on April 13 he signed a nonaggression pact with the Soviet Union. To Matsuoka, this meant that his country could now concentrate on its drive into Southeast Asia and its looming confrontation with the United States without worrying about an attack from the north.

Meanwhile, the Japanese prime minister, Prince Fumimaro Konoye, had initiated secret negotiations with the United States. Working through Admiral Kichisaburo Nomura, who had become ambassador to the United States in February, he informed Secretary of State Cordell Hull that Japan would be willing to negotiate all matters, including a withdrawal from China. But when Matsuoka returned from the Soviet Union, he dashed their hopes. Japan needs raw materials, he raged, and without expansion into Southeast Asia there would be none. Japan must build its empire, and the United States was interfering with these plans. Japan's future was with its allies, Germany and Italy, and only Japanese military strength, not negotiations, would put an end to American interference.

Still, on April 16, Hull asked Japan to give up its expansionist policies and to adopt the following principles:

Japan's foreign minister, Matsuoka, meets
Adolf Hitler and the German foreign minister
Joachim von Ribbentrop (at extreme left),
in Berlin in 1941.

1. Respect for the territorial integrity and sovereignty of each and all nations;

2. Support of the principle of noninterference in the internal affairs of other countries;

3. Support of the principle of equality, including equality of commercial opportunity;

4. Nondisturbance of the status quo in the Pacific except as the status quo may be altered by peaceful means.

Matsuoka's response to Hull's proposal was to submit, in May, two proposals of his own. These were as unacceptable to the United States as Hull's proposal had been to the Japanese. Matsuoka called for a Japanese-American neutrality pact, which, in effect, would have given Japan a free hand to conquer Southeast Asia. His second proposal called on the United States to stop aiding Great Britain and to pressure the Chinese to come to some sort of an agreement with Japan. This proposal also called on the United States to resume trade with Japan and to allow Japanese immigrants into the United States.

While proposals and counterproposals were flying back and forth between Tokyo and Washington, Japanese pilots began training for the anticipated assault on Pearl Harbor. This training intensified after the German invasion of the Soviet Union on June 22 totally removed the threat of a Soviet attack in the north. "Preparations for war with Great Britain and the United States will be made," was the directive issued by an Imperial Conference.

One month after the German invasion of the Soviet Union, Japanese troops occupied the rest of Indochina. American and British actions made this necessary, stated a Japanese Foreign Ministry dispatch: "Commercial and economic relations between Japan and third countries, led by England and the United States, are gradually becoming so horribly strained that we cannot endure it much longer. Consequently, our Empire, to save its very life, must take measures to secure the raw materials of the South Seas. . . . This is why we decided to obtain military bases in French Indo-China and to have our troops occupy that territory. . . ."

The American reaction to the Japanese takeover of Indochina was immediate. President Roosevelt ordered the National Guard of the Philippines into active service and put all American armed forces in the Far East under the command of General Douglas MacArthur. He froze Japanese credits in the United States, denied the use of the Panama Canal to Japanese ships, and halted the flow of raw materials, including gasoline, to Japan. The President told the Japanese to take their troops out of Indochina. He said that if they did so, the United States would help Japan obtain the raw materials it needed. But he also warned them of the consequences of attacking Dutch possessions in the East Indies. He threatened American action if the Japanese continued with its plan to take over Southeast Asia.

The American reaction to the Japanese takeover of Indochina intensified the debate between anti-war and pro-war groups in Tokyo. Many high-ranking naval officers were among those who had grave doubts about fighting a war with the United States. Foremost among them was Admiral Yamamoto, the formulator of the plan to attack Pearl Harbor. Yamamoto had gone to school in the United States and had served as the naval attaché in Washington. He had seen American industrial might firsthand, and the nation's industries were now engaged in arming the military forces. Yamamoto believed that Japan would win the initial battles, but he did not believe it could win a long war.

Japanese Admiral Yamanoto (left) is shown here with another high-ranking naval officer, Admiral Osumi.

In August, President Roosevelt and British Prime Minister Winston Churchill met aboard British and American Navy ships off the coast of Newfoundland. Here they formulated the Atlantic Charter, which denounced the use of force to take control of nations' territory and supported the right of people everywhere to choose their own form of government. Roosevelt and Churchill also discussed at length the Japanese takeover of Indochina. When Roosevelt returned from the meeting, he warned the Japanese that the United States would "take any and all steps necessary towards safeguarding the legitimate rights and interests of the United States and American nationals, and towards ensuring the safety and security of the United States."

With positions hardening, Japan stepped up its preparations for war. In early September the officers of Japan's First Air Fleet were told that "In case of war with the United States, Yamamoto plans to attack the U.S. Fleet in Pearl Harbor," and that they would carry out the mission. Immediately, study groups were set up by the First Air Fleet to answer these questions: What is the best route to Hawaii? What types of planes—and how many—would bring the best results? What type of training would be necessary? How can the fleet be refueled at sea?

Japanese Naval Intelligence also stepped up its quest for information. On September 24, the Japanese consulate in Honolulu was asked the following: "With regard to warships and aircraft carriers, we would like to have you report on those at anchor, tied up at wharves, buoys and in docks."

This message, like hundreds before it, was intercepted, decoded, and translated by United States Intelligence. In the summer of 1940, the Signal Intelligence Service had broken the Japanese diplomatic code and other codes. Since that time, all messages between the Foreign Office in Tokyo and Japanese embassies and consulates around the world, including Washington, D.C., and Honolulu, had been read by a few high-ranking American leaders.

But this message caused no particular concern. Many similar messages had been intercepted before, in Hawaii and in other places. Perhaps, it was thought, the Japanese were planning some sort of sabotage.

As Japan prepared for war, the United States pushed its factories to work overtime to produce planes, tanks, ships, guns, and other war matériel. When President Roosevelt ordered the Navy to "shoot on sight" any German submarines, most Americans supported him. They supported him, too, in his policy toward Japan. A Gallup poll taken in early September showed that 70 percent of the American people would "take steps to keep Japan from becoming more powerful even if this means risking war."

By early October, the militarists in Japan were on their way to gaining complete control of the government. On October 6, the Army High Command stated that "The Army concludes that there is no hope in conciliatory settlements of the Japanese-American negotiations. Therefore, war is inevitable. . . . If the Foreign Office believes that there is hope for conciliatory settlement, it may continue the negotiations with the deadline set at October 15." On October 16, Prime Minister Konoye resigned, and General Hideki Tojo, the war minister, took control of the government. Tojo, whose nickname was the Razor, was a blunt and outspoken advocate of war with the United States.

The following day, Ambassador Grew again warned Washington of the possibility of a sudden attack by Japan. Grew knew that, with Konoye's resignation, many others who were against war with the United States would also leave the government, and that the pro-war group, led by Tojo, would hasten their war plans.

Events did indeed move quickly. On November 5, Yamamoto issued Combined Fleet Operational Order No. 1. It detailed the full range of Japan's war plans. The American Pacific Fleet was to be destroyed, and the American lines of supply to the Far East would be cut. At the same time, Japan

would attack the Philippines, Malaya, Hong Kong, and Thailand. The Netherlands East Indies and Burma would be attacked next, followed by Guam, Wake Island, and Midway Islands.

Two days later, the Naval General Staff published an order that pinpointed the time and place of the attack on the United States:

1. The Task Force will launch a surprise attack at the outset of the war upon the U.S. Pacific Fleet supposed to be in Hawaiian waters, and destroy it.

2. The Task Force will reach the designated stand-by point for the operation in advance.

3. The date of starting the operation is tentatively set forth as December 8, 1941 (December 7, Hawaiian time).

Japanese spies in Hawaii had reported that the fleet usually returned to Pearl Harbor on Fridays, staying until Monday. December 7 was chosen because it was a Sunday and most Navy personnel would be ashore.

In the month before the attack on Pearl Harbor, the United States and Japan continued their negotiations. But both knew that the negotiations would be fruitless. The United States was playing for time—time for its military buildup. Japan was hoping to deceive the Americans so that its attack would be a complete surprise. In every war that Japan had fought—and won—beginning with the 1894–95 war with China, success had come as a result of a surprise attack.

Japan's war minister, General Hideki Tojo, headed his country's government during World War II.

On November 16, Japanese submarines began their long journey to Hawaiian waters. On the next day, the ships of the First Combined Fleet left Saeki Bay on Kyushu, Japan's southernmost island. Their destination was Hitokappu (Tankan) Bay in the Kurile Islands, a thousand miles (1,600 km) north of Tokyo. The fleet that would assemble in the Kuriles included Japan's six largest aircraft carriers, two battleships, two cruisers, and a number of destroyers, as well as oilers and supply ships. Aboard the aircraft carriers were more than 400 airplanes, including fighters, dive bombers, high-level bombers, torpedo planes, and air-patrol planes.

Even as the fleet was gathering, negotiations between Japan and the United States continued in Washington. And the United States continued to intercept and decode messages sent from Tokyo to the two negotiators, Ambassador Nomura and special envoy Saburo Kurusu, who had arrived in Washington on November 15. One message, intercepted on November 22, told Nomura that "There are good reasons . . . why we wanted to settle Japanese-American relations by the 25th . . . we have decided to wait until the 29th. This time we mean it; the deadline cannot be changed. After that things are automatically going to happen."

Thus President Roosevelt and Secretary of State Hull knew that the Japanese government was not negotiating in good faith. They knew that Japan was about to strike. Everyone knew this, but they did not know where the first blow would fall. Admiral Harold R. Stark, chief of naval operations, informed Admiral Kimmel in Hawaii that "a surprise aggressive movement in any direction including attack on Philippines or Guam is a possibility." Defenses in these areas had already been reinforced. Submarines had been stationed in the waters around Wake and Midway Islands. Marine strength on Wake and Johnston Islands had been reinforced. But in Hawaii the concentration was on the prevention of possible sabotage by Japanese living in the islands.

On November 27, the Navy Department sent another warning message to fleet commanders, including Admiral

Kimmel at Pearl Harbor. "This despatch is to be considered a war warning," the message read. "Negotiations with Japan looking toward stabilization of conditions in the Pacific have ceased and an aggressive move by Japan is expected within the next few days." The message listed the Philippines, Thailand, and Borneo as possible targets, but not Hawaii. Two days earlier, amid a swirling snowstorm, Japan's First Air Fleet had left the shelter of the Kuriles and begun its long and silent journey to Pearl Harbor.

The day before the Navy's war warning, Hull, in a Ten-Point Memo, demanded that Japan withdraw its military forces from China and Indochina. Tojo purposely delayed his response to Hull. He told Nomura and Kurusu to convince the Americans that negotiations would continue. Events now moved rapidly. On December 1, the Emperor gave his tacit approval of the war plans. Tojo then demanded and won the right to mount a surprise attack. Yamamoto wanted to give the United States ample warning, but he won only a small concession from Tojo: Secretary of State Hull would be notified at 1:00 P.M., December 7, Washington time, that Japan was breaking diplomatic relations. At 1:00 P.M. in Washington, it would be 7:30 A.M. in Hawaii—thirty minutes before the attack on Pearl Harbor and too late for the United States military to take effective action.

On December 3, the Japanese fleet refueled at sea after battling its way through a ferocious storm. On the 4th, Japanese consulates in Washington and elsewhere were told to destroy their codes and top secret papers; and on the 5th, Japanese officials in the United States were told to prepare to leave the country. Both of these messages were intercepted, decoded and translated by United States Intelligence services.

When President Roosevelt learned, on December 6, that Japanese forces were moving toward Indochina and Malaya, he sent a personal note to Emperor Hirohito, asking him to help "restore traditional amity and prevent further death and destruction in the world." Roosevelt's message did not reach the Emperor until after the attack on Pearl Harbor. Even if it had, events were beyond the Emperor's control. On that very day, the Navy intercepted Tojo's reply to Hull. The message, sent in fourteen parts, totally rejected Hull's Ten-Point Memo and placed the blame for the situation in Asia on the United States. When Roosevelt read the first thirteen parts of the message—the fourteenth part would not be decoded until the following morning—he said, "This means war."

It was now past nine o'clock at night in Washington—mid-afternoon in Hawaii. There, more than twenty Japanese submarines had taken up positions around the islands. And by the end of the day, the Japanese Fleet would be less than 400 miles (650 km) from Oahu.

CHAPTER

DECEMBER 7, 1941

At 5:50 A.M. on December 7, 1941, Hawaii was asleep; nearly one hundred ships of the United States Pacific Fleet were cloaked in darkness inside the protected waters of Pearl Harbor. But 220 (350 km) miles north of Oahu, the First Japanese Air Fleet was at its launch position. The fighter and bomber pilots had eaten a ceremonial breakfast and were checking and rechecking their planes. The crewmen were topping off the fuel tanks. At 6 o'clock, as the rough seas smashed at the ships' hulls, the first planes took to the air. By 6:20, all 183 planes of the first attack wave were airborne. After rendezvousing high above the fleet, the pilots headed their craft toward Oahu and Pearl Harbor. The flight would take them an hour and a half.

At almost exactly the same moment, in Washington, D.C., General George C. Marshall, United States Army Chief of Staff, sent a "war warning" to the Philippines, the Panama Canal, the United States west coast, and Hawaii. In Washington it was just before noon, and four and a half hours earlier the fourteenth part of the Japanese reply to Cordell Hull had been decoded. Hull was to be informed that "The Japanese Government regrets to have to notify the American Government that in view of the attitude of the American Government it cannot but consider that it is impossible to reach an agreement through further negotiation."

The response in Washington was muted. President Roosevelt commented that "it looks as though the Japanese were going to sever negotiations." Most of the military and political leaders in the nation's capital were of the same opinion. Japan did not declare war, nor did it threaten war. But no sooner had this Japanese note been read than a message to Nomura was intercepted. This one gave him specific instructions on when to deliver the Fourteen-Part Note: "Will the ambassador please submit to the United States Government (if possible to its Secretary of State) our reply to the United States at 1:00 P.M. on the 7th, your time." The significance of this time was noted immediately by Colonel Rufus S. Bratton, chief of the Far Eastern Section of the Army's Signal Intelligence Service. He saw that at 1:00 P.M. in Washington, it would be 7:30 A.M. in Hawaii—the perfect time for a surprise attack.

But Washington could still not accept the possibility of an attack on Hawaii. So Marshall's "war warning" was sent to a number of American military installations around the world. It warned that "The Japanese are presenting at 1:00 P.M., EST, today, what amounts to an ultimatum. Also they are under orders to destroy their code machines immediately. Just what significance the hour set may have, we do not know, but be on the alert accordingly."

Marshall's warning was sent almost immediately to the Panama Canal, the Philippines, and the west coast. But at that moment, poor atmospheric conditions made it impossible for the naval radio station to transmit the message to Hawaii. The decision was thus made to send it via Western Union, a commercial service that had a teletype link with Hawaii. The message, however, was not marked urgent. As a result, though it arrived in Hawaii just after 7:30 A.M., it was not delivered to General Short until 3 o'clock in the afternoon. At that time the Japanese Fleet, after a successful mission, was steaming back to Japan. Between the hours of 7:55 and 10:00 A.M., its carrier-based planes had knocked out nearly half of the United States Navy.

The first shot of the war between the United States and Japan was fired at 6:45 A.M., more than an hour before the Japanese planes filled the skies over Oahu. And the first loss of the war was suffered by Japan, not the United States. The *Ward*, a destroyer patrolling the waters outside of Pearl Harbor, was notified that a midget submarine was trying to sneak into Pearl Harbor in the wake of the *Antares*, a stores and supply ship that was towing a barge into the harbor. An antitorpedo net usually blocked the entrance to the harbor, but it had been opened to allow entrance to the *Antares*.

Lieutenant William Outerbridge was commander of the *Ward*. Naval orders stated that unidentified submarines were to be fired on, and this is what he did. The *Ward's* first shot sailed harmlessly over the Japanese sub, but the second shot smashed into the conning tower. Four depth charges finished the job, and the sub went to the bottom. At 6:51 A.M., Outerbridge radioed Naval Headquarters at Pearl Harbor, "We have attacked, fired upon and dropped depth charges upon submarine operating in defensive sea area." When this message reached Admiral Kimmel's office, his chief of staff, Captain John B. Earle, asked only that the report "be verified." No further action was taken, possibly because over the previous months there had been numerous reports of submarines in the waters around Pearl Harbor. Nevertheless, an opportunity to alert the fleet was lost—and the Japanese planes were but one hour away.

At almost the very same moment, another opportunity to alert the fleet was lost. On the morning of December 7, five Army radar stations were scattered throughout the island of Oahu. One of these was located about 25 miles (40 km) north of Pearl Harbor, near Kahuku Point, the northernmost tip of Oahu. Just after 7:00 A.M., the two Army privates who were manning the radar station, Joseph Lockard and George Elliott, saw several blips on the radar screen. The blips represented a flight of more than 50 planes—just 132 miles (212 km) away. Elliott called the Information Center at Fort Shafter. The officer who took the information was certain the blips

*A Japanese "Zero" fighter takes off from
the deck of an aircraft carrier bound for
Pearl Harbor on December 7, 1941.*

represented a flight of American B-17s coming to Hawaii from the mainland, so he told Elliott and Lockard, "Don't worry about it." At 7:40, the planes were less than 20 miles (32 km) from Oahu. At 7:49 they were over Oahu, and Lieutenant Commander Mitsuo Fuchida, leader of the first attack wave, gave the order to his pilots: "To! To! To!" (Attack! Attack! Attack!). The planes began to fan out toward their targets. Fifty-one fighter planes headed toward Wheeler Field in the center of Oahu's central valley and Kaneohe Naval Air Station on the island's east coast. Forty-nine high-level bombers raced toward Hickam Field, just east of the entrance to Pearl Harbor. And ninety-one torpedo bombers and dive bombers set their sights on Pearl Harbor.

Far below the Japanese pilots, and just five minutes away, thousands of unsuspecting American servicemen prepared to start their day. Some were just getting out of bed, others were eating breakfast or reading the Sunday newspaper. In the harbor, nearly one hundred ships of all sizes sat immobile in the calm waters. There were no aircraft carriers among them, because the three carriers of the Pacific Fleet were elsewhere. The *Enterprise* had been sent to deliver fighter planes to the Marines on Wake Island. The *Lexington* was delivering bombers to Midway Islands. And the *Saratoga*, in need of repairs, was on its way to California.

But every other kind of ship was there, including eight battleships—the backbone of the fleet—two heavy cruisers, six light cruisers, five submarines, twenty-nine destroyers, and two dozen auxiliary ships.

As Commander Fuchida viewed this scene, not a single American plane rose to meet him; not a single antiaircraft gun opened fire. He immediately radioed the fleet: "Tora! Tora! Tora!" (Tiger! Tiger! Tiger!)—the prearranged signal that meant complete surprise had been achieved.

And complete surprise it was. At Wheeler, Hickam, Bellows, and Ewa fields, Army and Marine planes were parked wing tip to wing tip in neat rows so that saboteurs would find it more difficult to get to them. At the Army fields, only four of the thirty batteries were in position—and they had no ammunition. And on the ships, fewer than two hundred of the eight hundred guns were manned.

The bombs began to fall on Pearl Harbor at five minutes to eight. One of the first hit Naval Air Headquarters on Ford Island, where officers were discussing the report of the sinking of the midget sub by the *Ward*. Soon explosions could be heard in every part of Pearl Harbor. Many people thought that an air raid drill was in progress. It took several minutes for people to realize that this was the real thing. The message went out to the fleet: "Air raid, Pearl Harbor. This is not drill!" The air raid would last for about two hours, and come in two waves. The first would last from 7:55 to 8:30 A.M.; the second, from 8:45 to about 10:00. At the end, half the United States fleet would be destroyed or out of commission for the better part of a year.

In Pearl Harbor, off the northeast shore of Ford Island, is Battleship Row. Here was moored the heart of the American Pacific Fleet, the battleships *Nevada, Arizona, Tennessee, West Virginia, Maryland, Oklahoma,* and *California.* Just east of Ford Island, an eighth battleship, *Pennsylvania,* was in dry dock, along with five cruisers. Japanese spies had pinpointed the location of each of these ships, and their intelligence reports had been memorized by the Japanese pilots, each of whom was given specific targets.

The first ship to be hit, the light cruiser *Raleigh,* was not in Battleship Row but moored off the northwest coast of Ford Island. When the Japanese pilots started their bombing run, the *Raleigh's* crew, like others, thought they were witnessing an air raid drill. Not until the planes got close enough for them to see the red balls—the rising suns—on the sides of the planes did they realize that Japanese forces were attacking, that war was upon them. The *Raleigh's* gunners managed to load some of the ship's antiaircraft guns and to fire at the incoming planes, but within minutes the ship was hit by a torpedo and started to list (lean to one side). Near the *Raleigh* was the *Utah,* a former battleship that was now used as a

These planes on Ford Island were among the first targets of the bombs that fell on Pearl Harbor.

target ship. Soon, a number of torpedoes would find her and send her to the bottom of the harbor, despite the fact that Japanese pilots had been told not to waste their torpedoes on this target ship.

One Japanese torpedo bomber now sought out the *Pennsylvania*, which was in drydock. When the pilot realized that his torpedo would be blocked by the mooring slip, he fired at the *Oglala*, a minelayer. Moored next to the *Oglala* was the cruiser *Helena*, and this one torpedo exploded between the two ships, severely damaging both.

It was not yet eight o'clock; the attack had been under way for less then five minutes. Admiral Kimmel was still in his quarters overlooking Pearl Harbor when he was told that ''There's a message from the signal tower saying the Japanese are attacking Pearl Harbor and this is no drill.'' Kimmel rushed outside where, from the lawn of a fellow-officer's home, he watched the destruction taking place in the harbor. He and the officer's wife, Mrs. John B. Earle, saw the *Arizona* hit by eight bombs and torpedos. The last bomb exploded deep within the forward magazine. As the munitions and a boiler exploded, flames shot into the air and fell on nearby ships, causing more damage to some ships than the Japanese had done with their bombs. ''The ship was sinking like an earthquake had struck it,'' one sailor later reported. Indeed, the *Arizona* went down so fast that hundreds of crewmen were trapped below. About twelve hundred sailors were killed on the *Arizona*, half of those killed in the entire attack.

Next to the *Arizona* was the *Vestal*, a repair ship. It had been hit by two bombs and was on fire. But the force of the blast from the exploding *Arizona* put out the flames and blew a hundred sailors overboard.

The U.S.S. Arizona
sank with 1,000
sailors on board.

Three torpedoes hit the *Oklahoma* at almost the same moment. Water rushed in through the gaping holes in her hull, and the ship began to list. The order to abandon ship was given, but as the men scrambled overboard, she was hit by two more torpedoes. The *Oklahoma* rolled over and sank. The scene was described by Mrs. Earle: "Then slowly, sickeningly, the *Oklahoma* began to roll over on her side, until, finally, only her bottom could be seen. It was awful, for great ships were dying before my very eyes! Strangely enough, at first I didn't realize that men were dying too." On the *Oklahoma*, four hundred men died. The survivors swam to the *Maryland*, which was moored inboard of the *Oklahoma*. This position protected the *Maryland* from torpedoes, but two bombs found their mark. The ship was damaged but it survived the attack.

As the *Oklahoma* was sinking, the ship just north of her in Battleship Row, the *West Virginia*, was hit by at least eight torpedoes and two bombs. It too sank to the bottom, taking 105 sailors down. Inboard of the *West Virginia* was the *Tennessee*. Protected from torpedoes by the *West Virginia*, the seamen of the *Tennessee* were able to loose a fierce barrage of antiaircraft fire before the ship was hit by two bombs.

At the southernmost end of Battleship Row stood the *California*. It was hit by a bomb and two torpedoes, one of which blew up the ship's magazine. Within two hours, the *California* would settle to the bottom of the harbor.

At the northern end stood the *Nevada*. Its gunners shot down two Japanese torpedo planes, but not before one of them scored a direct hit. Three high-level bombers also found their mark, and the *Nevada* settled to the bottom.

The *Pennsylvania*, a difficult target for the Japanese torpedo planes, was finally hit by both dive bombers and high-altitude bombers more than an hour after the attack had started. But the ship sustained relatively little damage. Near the *Pennsylvania*, however, three other ships were destroyed, all of them cruisers. The *Shaw*, *Cassin*, and *Downes* all blew up after bombs and torpedoes made direct hits.

Smoke fills the air over Pearl Harbor in the wake of the Japanese surprise attack.

On land the devastation was just as great. At Ewa Field, the Marine air base to the west of Pearl Harbor, thirty planes were destroyed. At Hickam Field, to the east of Pearl, more than fifty planes were destroyed. And on Ford Island itself, thirty-three patrol planes were destroyed. The Japanese did not neglect military installations away from the Pearl Harbor area. At Kaneohe Naval Air Station, on Oahu's east coast, twenty-seven planes were destroyed and six were damaged. Three planes that were on patrol escaped the carnage. At Wheeler Field more than sixty planes were destroyed, and several hundred soldiers were killed when a dive bomber scored a direct hit on a barracks. There was also widespread damage at Bellows Field on the southeast coast. In all, 188 Army and Navy planes were destroyed and 159 damaged.

The Japanese attack on Pearl Harbor and other military installations on the island of Oahu ended at about 10:00 A.M. By 11:00 A.M. all the Japanese planes were back on their carriers. Their losses: 29 planes, 1 submarine, 5 midget submarines, and fewer than 100 men.

The American losses were staggering: 18 major ships were sunk or seriously damaged: 188 planes were destroyed: and 2,403 people were killed, including 68 civilians. But it could have been worse. The three Pacific Fleet aircraft carriers were unharmed. And for some reason the Japanese had not attacked and destroyed the fuel-oil tanks at Pearl Harbor. Many repair ships and dry dock facilities were also undamaged. With aircraft carriers, ample fuel oil, and working repair facilities, the United States could prepare for the long road back from the humiliating defeat suffered at Pearl Harbor.

President Roosevelt learned about the Japanese attack on Pearl Harbor just fifteen minutes after it started. In Washington, D.C., it was 1:40 in the afternoon. Nomura and Kurusu, the Japanese envoys, were due to meet with Secretary of State Hull to deliver the Fourteen-Part message from Tokyo. Roosevelt called Hull at about 2:00 P.M. to tell him about the attack on Hawaii. The Japanese were late for their meeting with Hull, and when they were ushered into his office they immediately gave him the message. Hull pretended to read it over—he had read the entire thing already—and then looking at Nomura, he said:

> I must say that in all my conversations with you during the last nine months, I have never uttered one word of untruth. . . . In all my fifty years of public service I have never seen a document that was more crowded with infamous falsehoods and distortions—infamous falsehoods and distortions on a scale so huge that I never imagined until today that any Government on this planet was capable of uttering them.

A stunned and bewildered Nomura left Hull's office. He still knew nothing of the attack on Pearl Harbor, and would not learn about it until he returned to the Japanese embassy.

For the remainder of the day in Washington, Roosevelt met with the nation's military and political leaders. The question on everyone's lips was, "How could it have happened? How could the United States have been taken so completely by surprise?" Late in the evening, in Roosevelt's office, Senator Thomas Connally, chairman of the foreign relations committee, practically screamed at Secretary of the Navy Frank Knox: "Why did you have all the ships at Pearl Harbor crowded in the way you did?. . . I am amazed by the attack by Japan, but I am still more astounded at what happened to our Navy. They were all asleep. Where were our patrols?" The answers to these and other questions would have to wait. From December 22, 1941, until the year after World War II ended, eight different investigations would be held in an attempt to determine the reasons for the tragedy of Pearl Harbor.

But now, on December 7, President Roosevelt prepared his message to Congress, asking it to declare war on Japan. The nation was stunned, but it was also fighting mad. The crisis "had come in a way which would unite all our people," Secretary of War Henry Stimson had noted. Indeed, on December 7, 1941, the great debate between isolationists and their opposites ended. The political fighting between Democrats and Republicans ended. And 130 million Americans rallied as one. "Remember Pearl Harbor!" was their rallying cry.

CHAPTER VI

THE
UNITED STATES
AT WAR

The attack on Pearl Harbor was but one part of Japan's ambitious military plan. Even as the First Air Fleet attacked Hawaii, other Japanese planes bombed American installations in the Philippines and at Wake Island and Guam. Japanese ships shelled Midway Island, a naval air and submarine base 1,300 miles (2,100 km) northwest of Oahu in the central Pacific. In Southeast Asia, the Japanese invaded Thailand and Malaya, and before the end of December they would invade the Philippines and conquer Hong Kong.

The Japanese goal in Southeast Asia was to seize areas with abundant raw materials, but at Pearl Harbor and other American possessions the goal was to destroy American military might. The Japanese believed that with this accomplished there would be no nation powerful enough to deter them in their quest for an empire. While the Japanese reasoning was sound, at Pearl Harbor they committed a major strategic blunder.

When the Japanese planes disappeared from the skies over Hawaii at around 10 o'clock on the morning of December 7, the Americans there prepared for another air attack. Many also expected the Japanese to launch an amphibious landing in Hawaii—and there were many rumors about Japanese troops being seen in various parts of the islands. Many

Japanese officers had indeed urged that their planes be sent back to Pearl Harbor to inflict greater damage, but Admiral Nagumo had decided against this. This was a costly mistake for Japan.

Japanese planes had caused considerable destruction, but they had not destroyed a single American aircraft carrier and they had left intact the enormous stores of military fuel on Oahu. Had these fuel tanks been destroyed, the American Pacific Fleet would have been forced to retreat to the west coast of the United States. Admiral Yamamoto would later state, "Events have shown that it was a great mistake not to have launched a second attack against Pearl Harbor." His words were echoed by Admiral Nimitz: "The fact that the Japanese did not return to Pearl Harbor was the greatest help to us, for they left their principal enemy with the time to catch his breath, restore his morale, and rebuild his forces." The United States was now not only Japan's principal enemy— Congress declared war against Japan on December 8—but the principal enemy of Germany and Italy, both of which declared war on the United States on December 11.

World War II was now truly a global war, and the Axis Powers were clearly in the ascendancy. In Europe, every nation except neutral Spain, Portugal, Sweden, Switzerland, Ireland, and beleaguered Great Britain was under the heel of German troops. In the Soviet Union, German troops were at the gates of Moscow, but the Russians, on December 6, had mounted their first offensive since the German invasion on June 22. In Africa, the Germans, Italians, and Vichy French controlled most of North and West Africa. In the Pacific, the Japanese would, within six months, control an area that stretched from the Aleutian Islands in the north to the Netherlands East Indies in the south, and from the Marshall and Gilbert islands in the east to Burma in the west.

American entry into the war made it inevitable that the tide would turn against the Axis Powers. There were a number of reasons for this. First, the United States built one of the most formidable war machines in the history of warfare. Second, the nation's industries soon shifted to a war footing and produced the weapons of war in such quantities that they supplied not only America's fighting force of twelve million but also those of the nation's two principal allies, Great Britain and the Soviet Union. Third, American military and political leaders were astoundingly adept not only at conducting successful military operations in areas thousands of miles apart but at forging what was probably the most successful military coalition in history.

On the day that Japanese military forces attacked Pearl Harbor, there were 1.6 million men and women in the United States armed forces. This was the largest peace-time force ever maintained by the United States, and it was as a result of the 1940 Selective Training and Service Act. This act, the first peacetime draft in American history, had been preceded by two years of increased military preparedness by the United States.

The United States Pacific Fleet may have been caught unprepared at Pearl Harbor, but at President Roosevelt's prodding, the American military establishment had been improving its defenses ever since 1938. In that year, with Japanese forces winning control of northern and central China and Nazi Germany seizing control of Austria and part of Czechoslovakia, Roosevelt called for a 220 per cent increase in naval construction and the building of antiaircraft defenses in the United States. The pace of military spending increased again in 1939, after Roosevelt submitted a defense budget of $1.3 billion—15 percent of the national budget.

In 1940 Roosevelt requested $3 billion for defense and called for a 200-ship Navy, including seven battleships, that would be capable of defending American interests in both the Pacific and Atlantic. The buildup of personnel began on September 16, with the passage of the Selective Training and Service Act. The goal was the training of 1.2 million soldiers and 800,000 reservists. More than 16 million men between the ages of 21 and 35 registered for the draft. They were to serve for one year, but in August 1941 their service was lengthened to eighteen months, and as soon as war broke out this was extended to six months beyond the end of the war. In addition, the age limits were extended to include all men between the ages of 20 and 44. Later, the lower age level was made 18, but no men over the age of 38 were ever drafted.

From the beginning of the draft until the end of the war, 31 million men were registered and some 10 million were drafted. Volunteers raised the total number of men and women who served in the armed forces during the war to more than 16 million. Only the Soviet Union (22 million) and Germany (17 million) had more men under arms. And in terms of peak military strength, the American armed services (12.3 million) were almost as large as those of the Soviet Union (12.5 million). This maximum strength was attained in 1945, when the final battles of the war were being fought both in the Pacific and in Germany.

"In the space of three and a half years," wrote General Dwight D. Eisenhower, "the United States produced the fighting machine that played an indispensable role in beating Germany to its knees, even while our country, almost single-handedly, was conducting a decisive war against the Japanese Empire." This fighting machine—the Army (including the Army Air Force), the Navy, the Marines, the Coast Guard, and the more than 200,000 women who served in the Women's Auxiliary Corps (WAC), the WAVES, the Coast Guard SPARS, and the Marine Corps Women's Reserve— was the best-equipped military force in history. At its peak, the Army Air Force had nearly 80,000 planes, compared with 9,000 at the time of Pearl Harbor. And the Navy had 91,000 ships, 2,500 of which were warships, compared with fewer than 1,000 warships at the time of Pearl Harbor. The cost for this war matériel was staggering. From 1942 to 1945 the defense budget was $288.3 billion—48 percent of the entire national budget.

Most of this money was spent in American factories, and it was in these factories that the war was won. The industrial might of the United States was probably the most important factor in the Allied defeat of the Axis Powers.

On December 29, 1940, in one of his fireside chats, President Roosevelt had called on the nation to become "the great arsenal of democracy," and in the following spring the industrial plants began their shift to a wartime economy. On December 7, this shift took on a greater sense of urgency. The War Production Board and, later, the Office of War Mobilization oversaw an economy that produced war matériel on an unprecedented scale. In 1942, for example, Roosevelt had called on the nation's airplane manufacturers to produce 60,000 military planes a year, yet in 1943 they produced 85,000 and in 1944 the figure was 96,000. From the beginning of 1942 until the end of the war, total production was close to 300,000 military planes, with 34,500 of these going to the Allies.

Production was just as prolific in other areas. Under the direction of the Maritime Commission, shipyards turned out 71,000 naval and merchant ships. In a race against time, shipyards were turning out aircraft carriers in fifteen months and destroyers in five. Cargo ships were built in just seventeen days. More than 5,400 cargo ships were built during the war, 3,000 of them Liberty ships and the faster Victory ships. These ships carried millions of American troops and millions of tons of supplies to every part of the world. They carried Lend-Lease military equipment to Great Britain and the Soviet Union.

The shipyards also turned out new types of ships for the new types of warfare that Americans would face. Among these were the amphibious warfare ships that were so vital during the Normandy invasion and the island-hopping war in the Pacific. The landing ship–tank (LST) could carry twenty tanks ashore to establish a beachhead. The landing ship–dock (LSD) carried assault craft, and the landing ship–infantry (LSI) carried combat-ready infantry troops.

Automobile and truck factories manufactured 2.5 million

These airplanes represent part of the massive output of war matériel that United States industry produced in the years following Pearl Harbor.

military trucks during World War II, as well as 102,000 tanks and self-propelled guns. Munitions factories produced more than 20 million small arms and nearly half a million bazookas, an American-designed anti-tank weapon.

Most of this matériel was for American forces, but $50 billion worth of war goods, food, and clothing was sent to Great Britain, the Soviet Union, France, China, and other Allies under Lend-Lease.

The amazing accomplishments of American industry during World War II—between 1939 and 1945 the index of manufacturing increased by 96 percent—would not have been possible without the wholehearted support of the American people. Pearl Harbor had united these people in a way never before seen in American history, and there were few who did not contribute in some way to the war effort. With millions of men and women serving in the armed forces, there were, at first, labor shortages. But men came out of retirement to work in defense plants, and they were joined on the assembly lines by 3.5 million women.

Another factor in the accomplishments of industry was the close cooperation of industry and the scientific community. When the Japanese conquered Southeast Asia, the United States was cut off from supplies of many basic raw materials. A substantial portion of the oil used in the United States had come from the Netherlands East Indies. Shortages were overcome by increasing American oil production and by prevailing upon Venezuela to do the same. But the rubber shortage presented a different sort of problem, for there were no easy ways to obtain enough natural rubber to make up for the loss of supply from the Netherlands East Indies, from which the United States had obtained almost all of its needs. In one of the great stories of World War II, an entire new industry— the synthetic rubber industry—was created in a little over a year. By 1945 this industry was producing nearly a million tons of synthetic rubber a year from gasoline.

Scientists and American industry cooperated in many other areas to make the United States military the most effec-

tive fighting force during World War II. Among their accomplishments were advanced radar systems, the bazooka and other types of rockets, and the proximity fuse. And, of course, there was the atomic bomb, which was developed at a cost of $2 billion. On December 2, 1942, scientists produced the first controlled chain reaction, and in the spring of the following year work was started on the atomic bomb in Los Alamos, New Mexico. On July 16, 1945, near Alamagordo, New Mexico, a test bomb was detonated.

At this point in World War II, the war in Europe had been over for two months, but in the Pacific the United States and its Allies were faced with the need to invade Japan, where two million Japanese soldiers awaited them. It was feared that Allied troops would suffer hundreds of thousands of casualties in an invasion.

President Roosevelt had died on April 12, and his vice-president, Harry Truman, had assumed the presidency. The decision to drop the atomic bomb on Japan was his alone, although he did seek the advice of his political and military advisers. "Let there be no mistake about it," Truman wrote in his memoirs, "I regarded the bomb as a military weapon and never had any doubt that it should be used." And so it was used: the first bomb was dropped on the city of Hiroshima on August 6; the second was dropped on Nagasaki on August 9. Both cities were destroyed and tens of thousands of people were killed. Japan offered to surrender the next day, finally doing so on August 14.

The formal Japanese surrender took place on September

*Women welders in a Texas
aircraft factory painted death
masks of the axis leaders—
Mussolini, Hirohito, and Hitler—
on their welding hoods to
demonstrate their patriotism.*

2, 1945, aboard the American battleship *Missouri*. The surrender document, which ended the war that had begun at Pearl Harbor, was signed not only by Japan and the United States but by representatives from Great Britain, the Soviet Union, China, Australia, Canada, France, the Netherlands, and New Zealand. These were the nations—the Allies—that, along with the United States, had borne the brunt of the fighting against the Axis Powers.

During the three and a half years of World War II, the Axis Powers found it increasingly impossible to contend with the growing strength of the American military forces and with the prolific output of American industry. But there was another, no less important, factor in the Allied victory. The United States, because of its military-industrial might, and because of the leadership qualities of President Roosevelt, was able to forge the Allies into one of the most effective military coalitions in history.

Before the Japanese attack on Pearl Harbor and American entry into the war, those nations fighting the Axis Powers had a common enemy but they had no common plan to defeat it. England and France had made some attempts to coordinate their military and political activities, but this came to an abrupt halt with the fall of France in June 1940. When Germany launched its surprise attack on the Soviet Union on June 22, 1941, that country effectively became an ally of Great Britain, but Stalin's secretiveness and suspicious nature, as well as the fact that the two theaters of war were separated by more than a thousand miles (1,600 km) of German-controlled territory, precluded any effective military cooperation between the two nations.

American entry into the war changed this situation. To be sure, the Soviet Union continued to keep its Western Allies at arm's length, but United States cooperation with Great Britain and the Commonwealth nations resulted in the first coordinated effort to defeat the Axis. This effort, in fact, had begun eight months before Pearl Harbor. During March of 1941,

American and British military leaders had held a series of meetings and agreed that, should the United States be drawn into the war, the primary military thrust would be directed against Germany. The attack on Pearl Harbor did not alter this decision, even though the American people at this time overwhelmingly wanted prompt retaliation against Japan for its sneak attack on Pearl Harbor.

"Germany is still the prime enemy," Roosevelt assured Churchill. This position was, of course, wholeheartedly endorsed by the Soviet Union, where, at the time of Pearl Harbor, German troops held most of European Russia west of a line running from Leningrad in the north to Moscow in the center to Rostov and the Sea of Azov in the south. There were overriding military reasons for Roosevelt's decision to give priority to the war against Germany. "The European Axis," wrote General Dwight D. Eisenhower, "was the only one of our two separated enemies that could be attacked simultaneously by the three powerful members of the Allied nations, Russia, Great Britain, and the United States. . . . If we should decide to go full out immediately against Japan, we would leave the Allies divided, with two members risking defeat. . . . Meanwhile America, carrying the war alone to Japan, would always be faced with the necessity, after a Pacific victory, of undertaking the conquest of Hitler's empire with prostrated or badly weakened Allies."

From the beginning Germany was considered the most dangerous of the two major enemies. Its armed forces were substantially stronger than Japan's, and it had under its control the substantial industrial production and manpower of Europe. Further, the Allies believed that the Germans were capable of developing advanced and highly destructive weapons that could in time make impossible the liberation of Europe. In this belief the Allies were correct, but the German development of jet planes, rockets and nuclear power would come too late to prevent an Allied victory.

On the day before Christmas in 1941, Churchill met with

Roosevelt in Washington, D.C., and in a series of meetings that lasted until January 14, 1942, the two leaders restated the need to defeat Germany first and set up the Combined Chiefs of Staff Committee to direct the Allied war effort. The members of this committee were the British Chiefs of Staff and the American Joint Chiefs of Staff. The four able members of the American Joint Chiefs of Staff were: General George C. Marshall, chief of staff of the Army; Admiral Ernest J. King, commander in chief of the United States Fleet and chief of naval operations; General Henry H. (Hap) Arnold, chief of the Army Air Corps; and Admiral William D. Leahy, chief of staff for President Roosevelt.

General Marshall was one of the high-ranking military men who had been criticized for the total lack of preparedness at Pearl Harbor, but because of his skills as an administrator and strategist President Roosevelt had a great deal of confidence in his abilities to plan and direct the overall strategy of the war. Marshall had become Army chief of staff on September 1, 1939, the day World War II started in Europe. On that day, there were fewer than 200,000 men in the Army; by the end of World War II, there were more than eight million. At war's end, Churchill would call Marshall "the true organizer of victory."

Admiral King, an abrasive but highly intelligent naval officer, was named commander in chief of the United States Fleet early in 1942. He was appointed chief of naval operations at the same time, as well as a member of the United States Joint Chiefs of Staff. King was an expert on naval air warfare and during the war he would command the largest and most powerful naval force in history.

General Arnold, who was taught how to fly by the Wright brothers, commanded the Army Air Force during the war. He directed the daylight precision bombing of German cities and took personal command of the B-29s that destroyed many of Japan's industrial cities during the last months of the war.

Admiral Leahy, President Roosevelt's personal chief of staff, joined the Combined Chiefs of Staff in July 1942.

The United States also had strong civilian leaders, such as Secretary of State Cordell Hull, Secretary of War Henry Stimson, Secretary of the Navy Frank Knox, and Undersecretary of the Navy James Forrestal. But these men were overshadowed not only by the Joint Chiefs of Staff but by Roosevelt himself. Roosevelt ran the war, and the Joint Chiefs reported directly to him.

The first major decision of the Combined Chiefs of Staff Committee was to divide worldwide strategic responsibilities between the United States and Great Britain. Both countries were given responsibility for the conduct of the war in Europe, the Mediterranean, and the Atlantic. The United States took responsibility for the war in the Pacific, and Great Britain for the war in the Middle East and the Indian Ocean. Some of the United States' greatest military leaders were given specific areas of responsibility at this time. General Douglas MacArthur was chosen to command the Southwest Pacific area of operations. Admiral Chester W. Nimitz was put in command of all Allied forces in the rest of the Pacific. And in June of 1942, General Dwight D. Eisenhower took command of the European Theater of Operations. One indication of the quality of American leadership in these areas and of the unity of the Allies was the fact that there were very few instances in which Allied officers appealed the decisions of American commanders.

President Roosevelt and Prime Minister Churchill held their second wartime meeting in mid-June 1942, again in Washington, D.C. With them were the Combined Chiefs of Staff. The main topic of discussion was the first Allied offensive against the European Axis. But Churchill and Roosevelt could not agree. Roosevelt and the Joint Chiefs of Staff wanted to plan an offensive from Britain against German-held France, but Churchill and his military advisers felt that such an attack in 1942, without a massive military advantage over the defending Germans, could lead to a major defeat for the Allies or, at the very least, a long period of trench warfare similar to that of World War I.

Stalin, of course, was anxious for a second front because the Soviet Union was at this moment alone in the fight against Germany. The Joint Chiefs of Staff thus recommended to Roosevelt that if Churchill would not agree to an assault on France in 1943, the United States should turn all its military might against Japan, which, during the first week of June, had had its first taste of defeat at the Battle of Midway. Roosevelt, however, rejected this advice. Instead, he accepted Churchill's plan to invade those areas of North Africa that were controlled by Vichy France. Such an invasion would pit American soldiers against the European Axis for the first time, and it would prepare the way for an invasion of Italy. Churchill flew to Moscow to tell Stalin of this decision and to convince him that an Allied defeat on the beaches of France would be of little help to the hard-pressed Russian army. But Stalin was not easily convinced. He began to believe that the Allies would be pleased if Germany and the Soviet Union exhausted themselves on the battlefields of Russia.

Roosevelt, Churchill, and the Combined Chiefs of Staff next met in Casablanca, in January 1943. By this time Morocco, Algeria, and Libya had been freed from Axis control, but Tunisia would not be liberated until May. Roosevelt once again pressed for an attack across the English Channel into France, but Churchill insisted that after victory was won in North Africa, Sicily—and then Italy—should be the next target. Roosevelt finally agreed to an invasion of Sicily during the following June or July, despite the oppositon of the American Joint Chiefs of Staff. Both leaders also agreed that the bomber offensive against Germany would be intensified. It was at this meeting that Roosevelt and Churchill, to placate Stalin because the Normandy offensive had again been put off, agreed that the war could only end with the unconditional surrender of Germany.

It wasn't until May 1943, at their third conference in Washington, D.C., that Roosevelt and Churchill, on the advice of the Combined Chiefs of Staff, set the date for the invasion of France as May 1, 1944. At the same time, plans were made to step up operations against Japan. Once again Stalin was furious with the delay in opening a second front in Europe, and to make this known to Roosevelt he canceled a meeting that had been scheduled for the summer.

Allied forces invaded Sicily on July 9 and within two months Italy itself was invaded. Mussolini's downfall came quickly and his successor surrendered to the Allies on September 8. However, the war in Italy was far from over. Germany increased its troop strength there. At the same time the Russians were mounting a major campaign in the east. From this time on, the Germans were unable to mount attacks with sufficient force to stem the Russian Army.

Pleased now with the military advances of his Western Allies, Stalin agreed to meet with Roosevelt and Churchill at Teheran, Iran, in late November 1943. Here Roosevelt and, finally, Churchill agreed to give top priority to Operation Overlord—the invasion of France. Stalin in turn promised to mount a major offensive in the east that would coincide with the landing.

The landing at Normandy on June 6, 1944—D-Day—sealed the fate of Hitler's Germany. Bitter fighting would continue for eleven months, but one by one the countries of Europe would be liberated. The German High Command surrendered on May 7, 1945.

In the Pacific, the Americans had no disputes with their Allies, for they were completely in charge of this theater of war. A year before D-Day, United States forces had halted the Japanese advance at the Battle of Midway. By D-Day, MacArthur's forces were within striking distance of the Philippines, and Admiral Nimitz's forces had taken the Gilbert and Marshall Islands and were about to invade Saipan, an island that is only 1,500 miles (2,400 km) from Tokyo and from the Philippines. The invasion of the Philippines by the United States Sixth Army came on October 20, and by the end of February 1945 most of the fighting was over.

Iwo Jima, an island 775 miles (1,250 km) from Japan, was taken on March 16; the next step on the road to Tokyo was Okinawa. Okinawa is in the Ryukyu chain, and it is about 350 miles (560 km) from Kyushu, the southernmost Japanese home island. Okinawa was needed as an air and naval base to support the expected invasion of Japan.

The invasion of Okinawa began on April 1, 1945, and continued until the third week of June. It was one of the most bitterly fought battles of the war, with the Japanese using 400 *kamikaze* pilots in an effort to halt the American advances. About 13,000 Americans and 110,000 Japanese died during the battle for Okinawa. It was this battle, and the fanatical Japanese resistance, that helped convince President Harry Truman that the United States would suffer hundreds of thousands of casualties if Japan were invaded.

Truman, then, made the decision not to invade Japan but to use the weapon that had been developed under his predecessor, President Roosevelt. The use of two atomic bombs, one dropped on the city of Hiroshima on August 6, the other dropped on Nagasaki on August 9, ended for the United States the war that had begun nearly four years earlier at Pearl Harbor.

CHAPTER VII

PEARL HARBOR IN RETRO-SPECT

Pearl Harbor was—and is—
many different things to many different people. It was a
place-name synonymous with a date—December 7, 1941—
and it was an event synonymous with a phrase—"sneak
attack." It was a battle cry that united a divided American
people, and it was the subject of eight different investigations
that divided the American people over the placement of
blame for the nation's unpreparedness. Some even accused
(and still accuse) President Roosevelt of keeping knowledge
of the imminent attack secret so that the United States would
be forcibly drawn into the war against the Axis Powers.

But more than anything, Pearl Harbor was the turning
point of World War II. By bringing America into the conflict,
it guaranteed the defeat of Japan, Germany, and Italy and
thus ensured the survival of Great Britain and, very possibly,
the Soviet Union. "No American will think it wrong of me,"
wrote Winston Churchill, "if I proclaim that to have the United States on our side was to me the greatest joy. . . . So we
had won after all! Yes, after Dunkirk, after the fall of
France . . . after the threat of invasion . . . after the deadly
struggle of the U-boat war . . . we had won the war. England would live; Britain would live; the Commonwealth of
Nations and the Empire would live."

Stalin was not so effusive as Churchill, contenting himself at the Teheran conference with a toast "to American production, without which this war would have been lost." Indeed, American production gave the Soviet Union more than 400,000 trucks, 14,000 planes, 12,000 tanks, and other war goods worth more than $11 billion. And much of this aid was given in 1941 and 1942, when the Soviet Union desperately needed it.

Indeed, during World War II, the United States was the only nation that could have assured victory for the Allies. It alone had the skilled work force, the industries, and the raw materials necessary to manufacture the weapons of war with the speed and in the quantities needed. And perhaps because of its industrial might, the United States was also successful in creating an unusually successful coalition of nations.

CHRONOLOGY OF EVENTS

EARLY JAPANESE–
AMERICAN RELATIONS

1853   Commodore Matthew C. Perry sails into Tokyo Bay to force the Japanese to open their ports to trade with the United States.

1867   The United States purchases Alaska, annexes Midway Islands, and brings Hawaii into the American sphere of influence.

1895   Japan defeats China in a war and seizes Formosa.

1898   The United States annexes Hawaii and takes the Philippines from Spain.

1905   President Theodore Roosevelt arranges the Treaty of Portsmouth to end the Russo-Japanese War; the Japanese were victorious.

1910   Japan annexes Korea.

1914   Japan seizes the Marshall, Mariana, and Caroline Islands.

FROM ISOLATION TO
STEPS SHORT OF WAR

1922   At the Washington Naval Conference, the United States and Japan agree to limit naval strength.

1931   Japan invades Manchuria.

1936   Japan renounces the 1922 naval agreements.

1937   Japan invades China.

1938   U.S. Navy begins massive buildup.

1939   German armies invade Poland on September 1 to start World War II in Europe.

1940   German armies conquer most of western Europe; Japan signs a military pact with Germany and Italy and occupies northern Indochina; the United States introduces its first peacetime military draft and begins to aid Great Britain in all ways "short of war."

1941: THE BUILDUP
TO PEARL HARBOR

Jan. 27   Joseph Grew, U.S. ambassador to Japan, warns that the Japanese have a plan for a surprise attack on Pearl Harbor.

Mar. 11   President Roosevelt approves the Lend Lease Act.

Apr. 13   Japan signs a nonaggression pact with the Soviet Union.

Jun. 22	Germany invades the Soviet Union.
Jul. 24	Japan seizes the rest of Indochina.
Jul. 26	President Roosevelt freezes Japanese credits, halting trade with Japan.
Oct. 18	Japanese war minister General Hideki Tojo becomes premier.
Nov. 7	Japanese set December 7 as date for attack on Pearl Harbor.
Nov. 25	Japanese First Air Fleet leaves Kurile Islands for attack on Pearl Harbor.
Nov. 20	Ambassador Kichisaburo Nomura and special envoy Saburo Kurusu begin negotiations with U.S. Secretary of State Cordell Hull.
Dec. 6	President Roosevelt appeals to Emperor Hirohito to prevent further war.

DECEMBER 7, 1941

The Japanese attack Pearl Harbor, the Philippines, Wake, Guam, Midway Islands, Hong Kong, Malaya, and Thailand.

THE UNITED STATES
AT WAR

1941

Dec. 8	The United States declares war on Japan.
Dec. 10	Japan invades the Philippines, seizes Guam.

Dec. 11	The United States declares war on Germany and Italy.
Dec. 23	Japanese take Wake Island.
Dec. 25	Hong Kong surrenders to the Japanese.
1942 Feb. 15	Singapore surrenders to the Japanese.
Mar. 9	Japanese take the Netherlands East Indies.
May 20	Japanese conquer Burma.
Jun. 4–6	The United States defeats Japan in the Battle of Midway.
Jun.	Japanese complete conquest of the Philippines.
1943 Jan. 31	The United States defeats Japanese forces on Guadalcanal.
Mar. 2–4	Japanese fleet and convoy destroyed in the Battle of the Bismarck Sea.
Nov. 24	American forces take Makin and Tarawa in the Gilbert Islands.
1944 Feb.	American forces take Kwajalein, Truk, and Eniwetok.
Aug. 1	Americans take Tinian.
Aug. 10	Guam is recaptured.

Oct. 20	American forces invade the Philippines.
Oct. 23–25	The Japanese fleet is crushed at the Battle of Leyte Gulf.
1945 Mar. 16	Iwo Jima is captured.
Jun. 20	Okinawa is captured.
Jun. 30	The United States completes the reconquest of the Philippines.
Aug. 6	An atomic bomb is dropped on Hiroshima.
Aug. 9	An atomic bomb is dropped on Nagasaki.
Aug. 14	Japan surrenders.
Sep. 2	Japan signs surrender document.

FOR FURTHER READING

Bliven, Bruce, Jr. *From Pearl Harbor to Okinawa*. New York: Random House, 1960.

Borg, Dorothy, and Okamoto, Shumpei (eds.) *Pearl Harbor as History: Japanese–United States Relations, 1931–1941*. New York: Columbia University Press, 1973.

Dubofsky, Melvyn, *et al. United States in the Twentieth Century*. Englewood Cliffs, NJ: Prentice-Hall, 1978.

Feis, Herbert. *The Road to Pearl Harbor*. Princeton, NJ: Princeton University Press, 1950.

Freidel, Frank. *America in the Twentieth Century*. New York: Knopf, 1965.

Falk, Erwin A. *From Perry to Pearl Harbor: The Struggle for Supremacy in the Pacific*. Westport, CT: Greenwood, 1974.

Grew, Joseph C. *Ten Years in Japan*. New York: Arno Press, 1972.

Hoehling, A.A. *The Week Before Pearl Harbor*. New York: Norton, 1963.

Hull, Cordell. *The Memoirs of Cordell Hull*. New York: Macmillan, 1948.

Kahn, David. *The Codebreakers*. New York: Doubleday, 1967.

Kimmel, Husband E. *Admiral Kimmel's Story*. Chicago: Regnery, 1955.

Langer, William L. and Gleason, S. Everett. *The Undeclared War: 1940–41*. New York: Harper & Row, 1953.

Leckie, Robert. *The Story of World War II*. New York: Random House, 1964.

Lord, Walter. *Day of Infamy*. New York: Holt, 1957.

Millis, Walter. *This Is Pearl! The United States and Japan, 1941*. Westport, CT: Greenwood, 1971.

Prange, Gordon W. *At Dawn We Slept: The Untold Story of Pearl Harbor*. New York: Penguin Books, 1982.

Tamarin, Alfred. *Japan and the United States: The Early Encounters, 1791–1860*. New York: Macmillan, 1970.

Taylor, Theodore. *Air Raid—Pearl Harbor!* New York: Harper & Row, 1971.

Toland, John. *The Rising Sun: The Decline and Fall of the Japanese Empire, 1936–1945*. New York: Random House, 1970.

Wohlstetter, Roberta. *Pearl Harbor: Warning and Decision*. Stanford, CA: Stanford University Press, 1962.

INDEX